REDISCOVER ADVENT

MATTHEW KELLY

REDISCOVER ADVENT

ST. ANTHONY MESSENGER PRESS
Cincinnati, Ohio

Excerpts from *Rediscover Catholicism: A Spiritual Guide to Living with Passion and Purpose* (Cincinnati: Beacon, 2011) used by permission of Beacon Publishing. All rights reserved. Scripture passages have been taken from *New Revised Standard Version Bible,* copyright ©1989 by the Division of Christian Education of the National Council of the Churches of Christ in the U.S.A., and used by permission. All rights reserved.

Cover and book design by Mark Sullivan
Cover image © R Lemiengre | Veer

LIBRARY OF CONGRESS CATALOGING-IN-PUBLICATION DATA
Kelly, Matthew.
Rediscover Advent / Matthew Kelly.
p. cm.
Includes bibliographical references (p.   ).
ISBN 978-1-61636-164-8 (alk. paper)
1. Advent—Prayers and devotions. 2. Catholic Church—Prayers and devotions. I. Title.
BX2170.A4K45 2011
242'.332—dc23

2011021083

ISBN 978-1-61636-164-8

Published by St. Anthony Messenger Press
28 W. Liberty St.
Cincinnati, OH 45202
www.AmericanCatholic.org
www.SAMPBooks.org

Printed in the United States of America.
Printed on acid-free paper.

11 12 13 14 15 5 4 3 2 1

CONTENTS

INTRODUCTION

The past several years have been a tough time to be Catholic in America. In many ways this is a time of tragedy for the Church. The abuse of our children is a tragedy. The scandal of the cover-up is a tragedy. The fact that the entire priesthood has been tarnished by a small group of troubled priests is a tragedy. The absence of bold and authentic leadership is a tragedy. Morale is low and the number of Catholics leaving the Church is higher than ever before. The effects of all these tragedies are far reaching. They have left society at large with a very low opinion of Catholicism and caused many Catholics to be ashamed of the Church.

I have spent hundreds of hours reflecting on where we are in our journey as a Church, and one thing that has become startlingly clear is that we have forgotten our story.

Catholicism is more than a handful of priests who don't know what it means to be a priest. There are 1.2 billion Catholics in the world. There are sixty-seven million Catholics in America—that's at least fifteen million more people than it takes to elect an American president. And every single day the Catholic Church feeds, houses, and clothes more people, takes care of more sick people, visits more prisoners, and educates more people than any other institution on the face of the earth could ever hope to.

Consider this question: When Jesus was alive, where were the sick people? Were they in hospitals? Of course not; there were no hospitals at the time of Christ. The sick were huddled at the side of the road and on the outskirts of town, and that is where Jesus cured them. They had been abandoned by family and friends who were afraid that they would also become sick.

The very essence of health care and caring for the sick emerged through the Church, through the religious orders, in direct response to the value and identity that the Gospel assigns to each and every human life.

Allow me another question: How many people do you know who were born to nobility? Men and women whose parents are kings, queens, dukes, earls, duchesses, knights, and so on? Not many, I suspect, and probably none. Well, that is the number of educated people you would know if the Catholic Church had not championed the cause to make education available to everyone. Prior to the Church's introduction of education for the common man, education was reserved only for the nobility. Almost the entire Western world is educated today because of the Church's pioneering role in universal education.

The tragedy continues on another level as well. It is disturbing that at a time when millions of Catholics are angry and disillusioned with the Church there has been no significant effort to remind Catholics of who we really are, no strategic effort to raise our morale among Catholics, no organized effort to remind the world that, for the past two thousand years, wherever you find Catholics, you find a group of people making enormous contributions to local, national, and international communities.

We have spent more than two billion dollars settling lawsuits, but we have not spent a single dime on any special initiative to encourage Catholics in America to continue to explore the beauty of their faith. We have not spent a dime reminding the culture at large of the enormous contributions we make to society as a Church. We have not spent a dime inspiring Catholics at a time when more are disillusioned about their faith and the Church than perhaps ever before.

I am convinced of the following:

1. There is genius in Catholicism, if we will just take the time and effort to humbly explore it.
2. There is nothing wrong with Catholicism that can't be fixed by what is right with Catholicism.
3. If you and I are not part of the solution, we are part of the problem.

4. If sixty-seven million Catholics in the United States stepped it up a notch, something incredible would happen.

So let's decide, here and now, today, to begin to explore the genius of our faith, to be part of the solution, and to step it up a notch.

HOW TO USE THIS BOOK

This book is an attempt to raise morale among Catholics, to remind ourselves that there is genius in Catholicism, and to engage disengaged Catholics. It uses the Lectionary readings for Advent as a backdrop for the reflections, which were taken from the book *Rediscover Catholicism*.

The season of Advent is a time of expectation, when we prepare our home and our hearts to celebrate the birth of Jesus on Christmas Day. It is a season of hope, a time to nurture peace and experience joy in anticipation for the love that is made incarnate with the birth of Christ.

Each day, I encourage you to read the Scripture selections for the day, then the reflection that follows. Next, spend some time in meditation on the Scripture and on the reflection. Finally, there is an opportunity for prayer.

The prayers at the end of each day are related to a theme for the four weeks of Advent—hope, peace, joy, and love. These themes come from the Lectionary readings for the week, and reflect a particular virtue we can practice and adopt as we seek the unique gifts offered by the season of Advent. In the process, we will draw closer to God and find a richer expression of our faith. As well, we will explore what it means to be Catholic in this place and in this time.

Now is the time when we all need to rediscover Catholicism. I try to rediscover it every day, and when I seek in earnest to do so I am never disappointed. When I am able to set my ego and personal agenda aside, more often than not I am left in awe.

There are many people, Catholics and non-Catholics alike, who do not want to rediscover Catholicism. Others think religion—and Catholicism in particular—has no place in the modern context. I will admit that Catholicism is old. But let me ask you a question: If you had an ancient treasure map, would you throw it away just because it was old? No. The age of the map doesn't matter. What matters is whether or not it leads to treasure.

Catholicism is a treasure map: It may be old, but it still leads to treasure. Let's rediscover it together, and help others do the same.

Sunday of the First Week of Advent

YEAR A: ISAIAH 2:1–5; ROMANS 13:11–14; MATTHEW 24:37–44

YEAR B: ISAIAH 63:16B–17, 19B, 64:2–7; 1 CORINTHIANS 1:3–9; MARK 13:33–37

YEAR C: JEREMIAH 33:14–16; 1 THESSALONIANS 3:12—4:2; LUKE 21:25–28, 34–36

CHRIST IS THE WAY

. . . .

"I give thanks to my God always for you because of the grace of
God that has been given you in Christ Jesus, for in every way you
have been enriched in him, in speech and knowledge of every
kind—just as the testimony of Christ has been strengthened among
you—so that you are not lacking in any spiritual gift as you wait
for the revealing of our Lord Jesus Christ."

(1 Corinthians 1:4–8)

. . . .

REFLECTION

I believe God wants us to be happy. I believe God gave us this
yearning for happiness that constantly preoccupies our hearts. It

1

seems he has placed this yearning within each human heart as a spiritual navigational instrument designed to lead us to our destiny. God himself is the author of our desire for happiness.

The modern search for happiness is governed by individualism, hedonism, minimalism, and their fruits: greed, lust, laziness, gluttony, selfishness, exploitation, and deception. And yet, as these philosophies become more and more the focus of modern lifestyles, people seem to be filled with a greater discontent and unhappiness with every passing day.

As a father who takes a sincere and active interest in the lives of his children, God sent his only Son to respond to humanity's yearning for happiness, and to teach us how to satisfy that yearning. God sent his Son into the world to reconcile us with himself, certainly, but he also sent Jesus to show us how to live.

The philosophy of Christ is the ultimate philosophy of human happiness. It isn't just a way of life; it is *the* way of life. At the same time, the philosophy of Christ is one of self-donation. This is the great paradox of God's teaching. In our misguided adventures, we may catch glimpses of happiness as we live outside of the philosophy of Christ. You may even taste happiness for a moment living a life contrary to the philosophy of Christ, but these are stolen moments. They are just shadows of something infinitely greater.

MEDITATION

Where do I look for happiness in your life? How much of my search is directed toward what God has to give, and how much is directed toward what the world has to give? Does the balance need to shift?

PRAYER

The prayer for this week is based on Matthew 24:42–44: "Keep awake therefore, for you do not know on what day your Lord is coming… You must be ready, for the Son of Man is coming at an unexpected hour." Although it contains a warning to "keep awake," to remain alert, it offers hope and expectation in the coming of Christ at the end of time.

God of hope, I look to you with an open heart and yearning spirit. During this Advent season, I will keep alert and awake, listening for your word and keeping to your precepts. My hope is in you, as I wait to celebrate the birth of Jesus.

WALKING THE PATH OF CHRIST

. . . .

Many peoples shall come and say,

"Come, let us go up to the mountain of the LORD,

to the house of the God of Jacob;

that he may teach us his ways

and that we may walk in his paths.

For out of Zion shall go forth instruction,

and the word of the LORD from Jerusalem.

O house of Jacob,

come, let us walk

in the light of the LORD!

(Isaiah 2:3, 5)

. . . .

R E D I S C O V E R   A D V E N T

REFLECTION

Traveling the world I have learned that every faith community has problems and issues. Every Catholic diocese and parish in the world has difficulties. In some places, I have seen these problems drain communities of energy and enthusiasm, causing division and resentment. In other places, the same problems have given birth to renewed energy and enthusiasm, and indeed have become the source of increased unity.

What causes such varied outcomes in such similar situations? I have observed two differences. The first is on a very human level: Some people are willing to admit their mistakes and others are not. As a Church, and as local faith communities, we should always be willing to face our shortcomings with humility, courage, and hope. When we admit we have big problems, people start looking for big solutions.

The second difference is on a supernatural level: We should consider why problems occur in our lives and in the life of the Church. Do problems occur so that we can solve them? I don't think so. We are not here to solve the problems; the problems are here to solve us. This is one of the supernatural mysteries of our journeys here on earth.

When we approach any problem in the right way we become better-versions-of-ourselves. This is true for individuals, but it is also true for marriages, families, businesses, nations, and the Church.

MEDITATION

What shortcomings in my life are preventing you from walking in the way of Christ? How can I begin to make a change in these patterns or behaviors during this Advent season?

PRAYER

God of hope, I look to you with an open heart and yearning spirit. During this Advent season, I will keep alert and awake, listening for your word and keeping to your precepts. My hope is in you, as I wait to celebrate the birth of Jesus.

Tuesday of the First Week of Advent

ISAIAH 11:1–10; LUKE 10:21–24

SHOW ME, THAT I TOO MAY SEE

. . . .

Turning to the disciples, Jesus said to them privately, "Blessed are
the eyes that see what you see! For I tell you that many prophets
and kings desired to see what you see, but did not see it, and to
hear what you hear, but did not hear it."

(Luke 10:23–24)

. . . .

REFLECTION

More than ever, our non-Christian and non-practicing brothers and
sisters are sending you, me, and all of Christianity a message.
Though they are probably not aware of it, they are indirectly giving
witness to the Gospel. For within the message the people of our
times are sending us, there is a profound challenge for you and me
to embrace a life rooted more fully in the example and teachings of

Jesus Christ. Their message is clear, unmistakable, and disarmingly simple. Our siblings, parents, and children are sending us this message, as are our friends, neighbors, and colleagues. They are saying, whispering, crying out, "Don't tell me—*show* me!"

Their plea comes from a longing deep within them and represents their great hunger. They don't want to see another television evangelist, they don't want to read another book or hear another CD about Christianity, and they don't want to hear your amazing story of conversion. They want the real thing. They want to witness someone, anyone—just one will do—living an authentic life, someone whose words are supported by the authority of his or her actions. Someone striving humbly but heroically to live by what is good, true, and noble in the midst of—and in spite of—the modern climate.

They are not sending us this message merely to sound the childish cry of "Hypocrite!" Rather, theirs is a natural cry, a cry for help. They are saying to us, "Don't tell me—*show* me!" because they are so hungry for a courageous example of the authentic life, a life lived to the fullest, in this day and age.

MEDITATION

Does my life reflect what I believe about the Good News of Jesus Christ? This Advent, how can I begin to be a better witness of my Catholic faith?

PRAYER

God of hope, I look to you with an open heart and yearning spirit. During this Advent season, I will keep alert and awake, listening for your word and keeping to your precepts. My hope is in you, as I wait to celebrate the birth of Jesus.

Isaiah 25:6–10; Matthew 15:29–37

A HUNGER FOR MORE

. . . .

Jesus asked them, "How many loaves have you?" They said, "Seven, and a few small fish." Then ordering the crowd to sit down on the ground, he took the seven loaves and the fish; and after giving thanks he broke them and gave them to the disciples, and the disciples gave them to the crowds. And all of them ate and were filled; and they took up the broken pieces left over, seven baskets full.

(Matthew 15:34–37)

. . . .

REFLECTION

Our age seems to be governed by illusion and deception. We have built a whole culture based on appearance. Everything looks good, but scratch just below the surface and you will discover little substance.

This age, like any other, is made up of people like you and me. And if you listen carefully, if you look closely, you will discover that people are hungry. We were created to love and be loved, and there is a restlessness, a longing for more, a profound discontent with our lives and with our culture. We sense that something is missing, and deep within we know that nothing we can buy and no worldly pleasure will satisfy our restlessness.

This yearning preoccupies the human heart, and it is neither random nor accidental; everyone has it and we have it for a reason. The Holy Spirit (the "soul of our soul," as Pope Benedict XVI calls him) is at the source of these longings. It is the presence of God in the most interior part of ourselves that calls us to move beyond the surface concerns of our lives, to explore and experience something deeper.

Our hunger is not for appearances, nor is it for the fleeting and superficial; it is for something of substance. We are hungry for truth. The people of today are starving for the authentic, thirsting for the tiniest droplet of sincerity, aching to experience the genuine.

MEDITATION

For what do I hunger? How do the superficial things in life keep me
from reaching out to what will truly satisfy me?

PRAYER

God of hope, I look to you with an open heart and yearning spirit.
During this Advent season, I will keep alert and awake, listening for
your word and keeping to your precepts. My hope is in you, as I wait
to celebrate the birth of Jesus.

Thursday of the First Week of Advent

ISAIAH 26:1–6; MATTHEW 7:21, 24–27

TRUST IN GOD, OUR STEADFAST ROCK

· ·

Those of steadfast mind you keep in peace—

in peace because they trust in you.

Trust in the LORD forever,

for in the LORD GOD

you have an everlasting rock.

(Isaiah 26:2–3)

· ·

REFLECTION

In many things, perhaps in most things, the will of God is easily known. If we accept that we should love God and neighbor, a great many of life's choices become clear. If we accept that God has not created us to be some second-rate version of ourselves, but that God yearns for us to become the-best-version-of-ourselves, then a great

13

many more of life's choices become very clear—perhaps clearer than we would like. It is easy to see God's will in the context of his desire for us to become all he created us to be.

But there are some decisions, often the most important ones, that do not fall in either of these categories. And often, these are the biggest decisions of our lives. Perhaps you are deciding whether to be a nurse of a teacher. You can love God and neighbor in both of these professions. But which is God calling you to?

A priest once asked Mother Teresa if she would pray that God would give him clarity in a choice he had to make. She told him, "God may never give you clarity. All you can do is trust."

Sometimes we think we know for sure, sometimes we think we are pretty sure, and sometimes all we can do is trust. We can know that we are trying to love God and neighbor. We can know that a choice can help us become a-better-version-of-ourselves. We can know that a certain choice is a good fit for our legitimate needs, our unique talents, and our deepest desires. But we won't necessarily know that something is the will of God. Then, all we can do is trust.

MEDITATION

Is there a choice facing me now that requires trust in God? What choices have I made at other times, either in seeming certitude or in trust? How did these choices turn out?

PRAYER

God of hope, I look to you with an open heart and yearning spirit. During this Advent season, I will keep alert and awake, listening for your word and keeping to your precepts. My hope is in you, as I wait to celebrate the birth of Jesus.

WE ARE CALLED TO BE THE HOLY ONES

. . . .

Therefore, thus says the LORD, who redeemed Abraham,

concerning the house of Jacob:

No longer shall Jacob be ashamed,

no longer shall his face grow pale.

For when he sees his children,

the work of my hands, in his midst,

they will sanctify my name;

they will sanctify the Holy One of Jacob,

and will stand in awe of the God of Israel.

And those who err in spirit will come to understanding,

and those who grumble will accept instruction.

(Isaiah 29:22–24)

. . . .

REFLECTION

My experience has been that the great majority of Catholics do not know the goal of the Christian life. Others have cast the ideal aside, saying it is not conducive to modern living. Tragically, a great many have never heard it clearly articulated.

Holiness is the goal of the Christian life.

It seems to me that after the Second Vatican Council, and perhaps before, a great many educators and priests stopped teaching, preaching, and speaking about this goal. It seems they felt it was an unattainable ideal or simply unrealistic in the changing context of the modern world. They thought it made people feel guilty. They apparently wanted to make it easier for people. So they threw away or watered down the great goal of the Christian life.

The result, of course, was exactly the opposite of what they had intended. They didn't make it easier for people; they made it harder for them. Have you ever tried to find your way to a place you have never been before, with no directions, no map, and no clear description of the destination?

The authentic life orients us toward the goal of the Christian life. We are called to live holy lives, every man and every woman without exception, regardless of our age, color, socioeconomic background, or state in life. Living holy lives is the goal of the Christian life and our essential purpose.

MEDITATION

Do I see my life as holy? What are the signposts that guide me on my quest to live an authentic life?

PRAYER

God of hope, I look to you with an open heart and yearning spirit. During this Advent season, I will keep alert and awake, listening for your word and keeping to your precepts. My hope is in you, as I wait to celebrate the birth of Jesus.

Saturday of the First Week of Advent

ISAIAH 30:19–21, 23–26; MATTHEW 9:35—10:1, 6–8

PROCLAIM THE GOOD NEWS!

Then Jesus summoned his twelve disciples and gave them authority
over unclean spirits, to cast them out, and to cure every disease
and every sickness. Go to the lost sheep of the house of Israel. As
you go, proclaim the good news, "The kingdom of heaven has
come near." Cure the sick, raise the dead, cleanse the lepers, cast
out demons. You received without payment; give without payment.

(Matthew 10:1, 6–8)

REFLECTION

There are a great many people who think the problem with the world
today is that people don't come to church. They think the challenge
is to bring people to church, but the real challenge is to bring the
Church to the people.

Fundamentally, we are failing to do as Christ did—namely, to reach out and meet people where they are in their need, in their brokenness. We are failing to carry out the mission Christ entrusted to us through our apostolic lineage (cf. Matthew 28:16–20). We are failing to carry out the mission of the Church, which is to proclaim the good news of the Gospel to the people of every age.

If people do not come to church it is not their failure alone; it is ours as well. We should ask ourselves, "Why are they not coming to church?" People don't come to church because they don't see the value in it. If we convinced them of the value, if they really understood the richness and beauty of Catholicism, they would make church an indispensable part of their lives.

Engaging people means showing them how the Gospel can transform their lives. It means showing people that embracing the life God calls us to will liberate them from feeling torn in a dozen different directions. Engaging people means showing them how God intends to make their lives better.

MEDITATION

Who do I know that may need me, right now, to show them how the Gospel can transform their life? How can I reach out to that person (or persons) in his or her need?

PRAYER

God of hope, I look to you with an open heart and yearning spirit. During this Advent season, I will keep alert and awake, listening for your word and keeping to your precepts. My hope is in you, as I wait to celebrate the birth of Jesus.

THE ROAD MAP FOR LIVING AN AUTHENTIC LIFE

· ·

What sort of persons ought you to be in leading lives of holiness and godliness, waiting for and hastening the coming of the day of God, because of which the heavens will be set ablaze and dissolved, and the elements will melt with fire? But, in accordance with his promise, we wait for new heavens and a new earth, where righteousness is at home. Therefore, beloved, while you are waiting for these things, strive to be found by him at peace, without spot or blemish.

(2 Peter 3:11–14)

· ·

REFLECTION

Catholicism is a dynamic way of life that encourages and empowers each individual to become the-best-version-of-himself or herself. Quite different from the pop psychology and secular philosophies of our time, this is not something we do to and for ourselves (self-help), but rather something that takes place in and through Jesus Christ. We may be able to help ourselves to a certain extent, but it is precisely because we cannot help ourselves to the extent that we need and desire that we need a savior.

The Catholic lifestyle, when it is authentically presented and embraced, promotes the integration of every aspect of our daily lives and every aspect of the human person. And as you journey toward your destiny, God intertwines your talents with the needs of others to allow you the privilege of touching them, serving them, and inspiring them as they make their own journey.

Catholicism is a way of life in which the giving and receiving happen in equal measure. It nurtures the individual, the local community, and the whole human family. It affects every area of our lives

and is a guiding light in all of our decisions. Catholicism is a call to
live an authentic life. When embraced as a lifestyle it causes the ele-
vation of every human activity. Catholicism provides the map and the
tools for bringing each person into harmony with self, God, and
others.

MEDITATION

Do I see Catholicism as a once a week practice, or as an integral part
of my life? What steps do I need to take to embrace Catholicism as
my lifestyle?

PRAYER

*The prayer for this week is based on Isaiah 40:1–2, 10–11: "Comfort, O
comfort my people, says your God. / Speak tenderly to Jerusalem, and cry
to her / that she has served her term, that her penalty is paid, / that she
has received from the LORD'S hand double for all her sins. / See, the LORD
GOD comes with might, and his arm rules for him; / his reward is with him,
and his recompense before him. / He will feed his flock like a shepherd; he
will gather the lambs in his arms, / and carry them in his bosom, and*

gently lead the mother sheep." The theme is peace—not the peace of humankind but that which can only come from God.

God of peace, you watch over me with a tender love that is deep and true. This Advent, as I struggle with my human faults and failings, let me seek comfort in you and be reconciled in your peace. My soul rests in your goodness and mercy.

THE SEARCH FOR HAPPINESS

. . . .

The wilderness and the dry land shall be glad,

the desert shall rejoice and blossom;

like the crocus it shall blossom abundantly,

and rejoice with joy and singing.

The glory of Lebanon shall be given to it,

the majesty of Carmel and Sharon.

They shall see the glory of the LORD,

the majesty of our God.

(Isaiah 35:1–2)

. . . .

REFLECTION

It should come as no surprise to us that in this modern environment
the relevance of Jesus is being undermined and questioned. The

26

reason is simple: The philosophy of Christ is very different from the prevailing philosophies of our modern culture. In fact, they are completely opposed to each other. And yet, the teachings of Christ and these modern philosophies both claim to be the key to the fulfillment of a yearning that is common to us all.

The human heart is on a quest for happiness. Every person yearns for happiness like the desert yearns for rain. You have a desire for happiness; I have a desire for happiness. This desire is universal, common to every member of the human family. We simply desire to be happy, and we act from this desire.

We often do things that we think will make us happy, only to discover that they end up making us miserable. This is often because we confuse pleasure with happiness. And sometimes long-term misery comes disguised as short-term pleasure. Under the influence of philosophies such as individualism, hedonism, and minimalism, we often seek the happiness we desire through pleasure, possessions, power, and the path of least resistance. Each of these may offer moments of happiness, but they end too soon, having lasted ever so briefly, and our quest for a lasting happiness continues. These moments of happiness are of course real, but only as real as a shadow: A person's shadow is real, but it is nothing compared to the actual person.

So many of us spend a large portion of our lives chasing shadows.

MEDITATION

What brings me the most happiness in my life right now? Are these things shadows, or are they one with the teachings and philosophy of Christ?

PRAYER

God of peace, you watch over me with a tender love that is deep and true. This Advent, as I struggle with my human faults and failings, let me seek comfort in you and be reconciled in your peace. My soul rests in your goodness and mercy.

Tuesday of the Second Week of Advent

ISAIAH 40:1–11; MATTHEW 18:12–14

LOST AND FOUND

. . . .

If a shepherd has a hundred sheep, and one of them has gone
astray, does he not leave the ninety-nine on the mountains and go
in search of the one that went astray? And if he finds it, truly I tell
you, he rejoices over it more than over the ninety-nine that never
went astray. So it is not the will of your Father in heaven that one
of these little ones should be lost.

(Matthew 18:12–14)

. . . .

REFLECTION

Christ came to reconcile us with the Father, and in doing so, offered
the satisfaction of this craving for happiness that preoccupies our
human hearts. Love is our origin and our destiny. Our yearning for
happiness is a yearning for love. Created to love and be loved, we

seek out the fulfillment of our purpose. "God is love" (1 John 4:8), and our yearning for happiness is ultimately a yearning for God.

The *Catechism of the Catholic Church* wastes no time in addressing this truth. The opening point of chapter one, section one, reads, "The desire for God is written in the human heart, because man is created by God and for God; and God never ceases to draw man to himself. Only in God will man find the truth and happiness he never stops yearning for."

Our desire for happiness is part of the human condition. Our quest for happiness is a quest for God. It is the ultimate homing device, designed to draw us gently toward our eternal home. God creates us, places this desire within us, and sends us out into the universe. He does this knowing that sooner or later, if we can muster even the tiniest droplet of humility, the desire for happiness will lead us back to him—for no one else and nothing else can satisfy it.

Our yearning for happiness is a yearning for union with our Creator. Augustine's words echo anew in every place, in every time, and in every heart: "Our hearts are restless until they rest in you, Lord."

MEDITATION

When did I feel lost, directionless? Was God present in finding my way back? Where did I see God searching for me?

PRAYER

God of peace, you watch over me with a tender love that is deep and true. This Advent, as I struggle with my human faults and failings, let me seek comfort in you and be reconciled in your peace. My soul rests in your goodness and mercy.

Wednesday of the Second Week of Advent

ISAIAH 40:35–31; MATTHEW 11:28–30

"TAKE MY YOKE UPON YOU"

. . . .

"Come to me, all you that are weary and are carrying heavy burdens, and I will give you rest. Take my yoke upon you, and learn from me; for I am gentle and humble in heart, and you will find rest for your souls. For my yoke is easy, and my burden is light."

(Matthew 11:28–30)

. . . .

REFLECTION

The philosophy of Christ is based on discipline, but our modern culture abhors and has rejected discipline with all its strength. It is true that Jesus came to comfort the afflicted, but as Dorothy Day—journalist, social activist, and Catholic convert—pointed out, he also came to afflict the comfortable. The saints make many modern Catholics uncomfortable because they challenge us to throw off the spirit of the world and embrace the Spirit of God. Like Jesus, by their example the saints invite us to a life of discipline.

Contrary to popular opinion, discipline doesn't stifle or restrict the human person. Discipline isn't something invented by the Church to control or manipulate the masses, nor is it the tool that unjust tyrants and dictators use to make people do things they don't want to do. All these are the lies of a culture completely absorbed in a philosophy of instant gratification.

Discipline is the faithful friend who will introduce you to your true self. Discipline is the worthy protector who will defend you from your lesser self. And discipline is the extraordinary mentor who will challenge you to become the-best-version-of-yourself and all God created you to be.

As loyal and as life-giving as discipline may be, its presence in our lives is dwindling. Whether we are aware of it or not we are becoming spiritually ill without it. God has placed you here for some purpose, but without discipline, you will never discover that purpose. Without disciple you will march slowly and surely to join the masses who, in the words of Henry David Thoreau, lead lives of quiet desperation.

MEDITATION

What burden do I need to give to Jesus? Am I willing to embrace his yoke through a life of discipline and faithful practice?

PRAYER

God of peace, you watch over me with a tender love that is deep and true. This Advent, as I struggle with my human faults and failings, let me seek comfort in you and be reconciled in your peace. My soul rests in your goodness and mercy.

Thursday of the Second Week of Advent
ISAIAH 41:13–20; MATTHEW 11:11–15

TAKING CARE OF THOSE IN NEED

· ·

When the poor and needy seek water,

and there is none,

and their tongue is parched with thirst,

I the LORD will answer them,

I the God of Israel will not forsake them.

. . .

I will put in the wilderness the cedar,

the acacia, the myrtle, and the olive;

I will set in the desert the cypress,

the plane and the pine together,

so that all may see and know,

all may consider and understand,

that the hand of the LORD has done this,

the Holy One of Israel has created it.

(Isaiah 41:17, 19–20)

· ·

REFLECTION

Beyond our national and global impact, the local contribution Catholics make in every community, on a daily basis, is nothing short of remarkable. Every city and town has its own stories, but allow me just one example to make my point. In Chicago there are hundreds of Catholic organizations that serve the needs of the people of that city. One of those organizations is Catholic Charities. In a recent year the local chapter of Catholic Charities in Chicago provided 2.2 million free meals to the hungry and the needy in that area—that's 6,027 meals a day. It's an extraordinary contribution to the poor in Chicago.

Now imagine a large billboard on any of Chicago's busy, backed-up freeways. No photos would be required, just this simple text: *This year Catholic Charities will provide 2.2 million free meals to the hungry and the needy of Chicago. We don't ask them if they are Catholic—we just ask them if they are hungry. Rediscover Catholicism.*

The point is we have forgotten our story, and in doing so, we have allowed the world to forget it as well. We have allowed the anti-Catholic segments of the media to distort our story on a daily basis.

Our history is not without blemish; our future will not be without blemish. But our contribution is unmatched, and today, it's needed more than ever before.

MEDITATION

What are some of the Catholic stories in my community—in my home, parish, town, or state? What part do I play in shaping these stories?

PRAYER

God of peace, you watch over me with a tender love that is deep and true. This Advent, as I struggle with my human faults and failings, let me seek comfort in you and be reconciled in your peace. My soul rests in your goodness and mercy.

WHAT ABOUT THE CHILDREN?

· ·

But to what will I compare this generation? It is like children sitting in the marketplaces and calling to one another, "We played the flute for you, and you did not dance; we wailed, and you did not mourn." Yet wisdom is vindicated by her deeds.

(Matthew 11:16–17, 19)

· ·

REFLECTION

I have noticed that one element of our lifestyles that is propelling the modern madness is the number of activities that children are involved in today. Mothers have become taxi drivers. They go from school to tennis, to soccer, to ballet, to football, to piano lessons, to basketball, to the drive-through at McDonald's, to choir, to baseball, and so on.

Perhaps it is time we stopped and asked ourselves why our children participate in these activities. Are they just another form of entertainment? Are they a measure of our children's social status? Or are they directed toward some meaningful contribution to the development and education of our children?

I propose that if these activities are to have any real value in the education and development of a child, it will be because a child learns the art of discipline through these activities. And I assure you, our children will never learn the art of discipline while they are switching from one activity to another with great regularity. The overwhelming number of activities our children are engaged in is serving only to distract them from acquiring any real discipline in their lives, and as a result they are being firmly grounded in the superficiality that is ruling our age.

The purpose of education and extracurricular activities is to provide opportunities for our children to develop discipline. Once discipline is learned, it can be applied to any area of life. Those who develop this discipline go off in search of excellence and live richer, more abundant lives. Those who do not find this grounding in discipline may do many things, but none well.

MEDITATION

(If you have children) Are the activities of my children being directed toward a higher purpose, or are they just a means to pass time? *(If you don't have children or if they are grown)* What activities am I involved with, and towards what are they directed?

PRAYER

God of peace, you watch over me with a tender love that is deep and true. This Advent, as I struggle with my human faults and failings, let me seek comfort in you and be reconciled in your peace. My soul rests in your goodness and mercy.

Saturday of the Second Week of Advent

SIRACH 48:1–4, 9–11; MATTHEW 17:9A, 10–13

AS CHURCH, WE WORK TO FULFILL OUR DESTINY

. . . .

And the disciples asked him, "Why, then, do the scribes say that Elijah must come first?" He replied, "Elijah is indeed coming and will restore all things; but I tell you that Elijah has already come, and they did not recognize him, but they did to him whatever they pleased. So also the Son of Man is about to suffer at their hands."

(Matthew 17:10–12)

. . . .

REFLECTION

It is the task of the Church to introduce us to our destiny by unveiling for us the mystery of God, who is our ultimate end and our destiny. By "the task of the Church" I do not mean the job of your priest and your bishop and the parish staff. You and I have as much a role to play in the Church as any other member. Your role may be different from mine or a priest's, but it's no less important. What is critical is that each part of the one body fulfills its role to the best of his or her ability.

Allow me to rearticulate my last point in this way: It is your task and mine to introduce others to their destiny by unveiling the mystery of God for them. It is your task and mine to assist all those who cross our paths to fulfill their destiny. Serving others in this way will also allow us to fulfill our own destiny. This is one of the brilliant and beautiful ways that God has tied us all together.

By embracing the adventure of salvation we become with each effort more perfectly the person God created us.to be. Christ has commissioned the Church to guide and direct each of us along this path. Our dialogue and interaction with the Church is designed to help us hear the voice of God in our lives, live the life God invites us to live, and become the-best-version-of-ourselves. Let us never forget that people do not exist for the Church—the Church exists for people.

MEDITATION

What is my destiny? How can I unveil the mystery of God for someone else, and help them find their destiny?

PRAYER

God of peace, you watch over me with a tender love that is deep and true. This Advent, as I struggle with my human faults and failings, let me seek comfort in you and be reconciled in your peace. My soul rests in your goodness and mercy.

YEAR A: ISAIAH 35:1–6A, 10; JAMES 5:7–10; MATTHEW 11:2–11

YEAR B: ISAIAH 61:1–2A, 10–11; 1 THESSALONIANS 5:16–24; JOHN 1:6–8, 19–28

YEAR C: ZEPHANIAH 3:14–18A; PHILIPPIANS 4:4–7; LUKE 3:10–18

A DEEP PLACE OF PRAYER

· ·

John said, "I am the voice of one crying out in the wilderness,
'Make straight the way of the Lord,' as the prophet Isaiah said. I
baptize with water. Among you stands one whom you do not
know, the one who is coming after me; I am not worthy to untie
the thong of his sandal."

(John 1:23, 26–27)

· ·

REFLECTION

Did you ever see Pope John Paul II pray? Each morning, he cele-
brated Mass in his private chapel with about twenty guests. Perhaps
you were fortunate enough to attend. If not, perhaps you saw television footage of these Masses.

When this man knelt down to pray after Communion, he would close his eyes and go to a place deep within himself. Once he was there, nothing and no one could distract him. He would go to that place deep within himself, and from that place he brought forth the the fruit of his life: wisdom, compassion, generosity, understanding, patience, courage, insight, forgiveness, humility, and a love so apparent you could almost touch it.

The amazing thing is, if you put this same man in a football stadium with a hundred thousand people and a million more distractions, he still knelt down after Communion, closed his eyes, and went to that place deep within him where he connected with God. He allowed nothing to distract him from his prayer. It was from that place that he lived his life.

Find that place within you. If you do nothing else in your life, find that place and start to live your life from there. I pray I can visit that place within me and go there more and more frequently.

MEDITATION

Do I make time for prayer each day? What are some ways I can focus more on God and deepen my prayer?

PRAYER

The prayer for this week is based on 1 Thessalonians 5:16–22: "Rejoice always, pray without ceasing, give thanks in all circumstances; for this is the will of God in Christ Jesus for you. Do not quench the Spirit. Do not despise the words of prophets, but test everything; hold fast to what is good; abstain from every form of evil." Clearly, the theme is joy, and as we await the celebration of the birth of Jesus, our hearts are filled with hope and expectation for the coming of the Word made flesh.

God of joy, during these sometimes busy days of Advent, I keep your presence before my eyes. My heart is filled with joy for all you have done. You know the very depths of my soul, yet you love me with a tenderness that is beyond compare.

Monday of the Third Week of Advent

NUMBERS 24: 2–7, 15–17; MATTHEW 21: 23–27

THE AUTHORITY OF JESUS CHRIST

. . . .

The chief priests and the elders of the people came to Jesus as he was teaching, and said, "By what authority are you doing these things, and who gave you this authority?" Jesus said to them, "I will also ask you one question; if you tell me the answer, then I will also tell you by what authority I do these things. Did the baptism of John come from heaven, or was it of human origin?" They answered Jesus, "We do not know." And he said to them, "Neither will I tell you by what authority I am doing these things.

(Matthew 21:23–25, 27)

. . . .

REFLECTION

The life of Jesus Christ is indelibly engraved upon history; neither the erosion of time nor the devastation and compounding effects of

47

evil have been able to erase his influence. Some people thought he was crazy; others considered him a misfit, a troublemaker, a rebel. He was condemned as a criminal, yet his life and teachings reverberate throughout history. You can praise him, disagree with him, quote him, disbelieve him, glorify him, or vilify him. About the only thing you cannot do is ignore him, and that is a lesson that every age learns in its own way.

You can't ignore Jesus because he changed things. He is the single greatest agent of change in human history. He made the lame walk, taught the simple, set captives free, gave sight to the blind, fed the hungry, healed the sick, comforted the afflicted, afflicted the comfortable, and in all of these, captured the imagination of every generation.

His teachings are not complex or exclusive, but simple and applicable to everyone, everywhere, in every time in history, regardless of age, color, or state in life. It is the Gospel, the good news. Within it and through it we find salvation. Part of that salvation is happiness—not the foolish, empty happiness that this modern age associates with getting what you want. But rather, a happiness deeper and higher than any we could imagine or design for ourselves.

MEDITATION

How do I see Jesus—as a friend, teacher, spiritual director, role model? How has my relationship with Jesus affected my life?

PRAYER

God of joy, during these sometimes busy days of Advent, I keep your presence before my eyes. My heart is filled with joy for all you have done. You know the very depths of my soul, yet you love me with a tenderness that is beyond compare.

BLESSED ARE THE HUMBLE

. . . .

For I will leave in the midst of you

a people humble and lowly.

They shall seek refuge in the name of the LORD—

the remnant of Israel;

they shall do no wrong

and utter no lies,

nor shall a deceitful tongue

be found in their mouths.

Then they will pasture and lie down,

and no one shall make them afraid.

(Zephaniah 3:12–13)

. . . .

REFLECTION

One of my favorite passages from the Bible affirms my belief that the will of God is not as much of a mystery as we make it out to be. It comes from the book of Micah: "He has told you, O mortal, what is good; / and what does the LORD require of you / but to do justice, and to love kindness, / and walk humbly with your God." (Micah 6:8)

The prophet speaks of walking humbly with God. It is cited last, but it is in fact primary, because it is walking humbly with God that makes justice and love possible in our lives. Without God alive within us and working through us, you and I would not be capable of love or justice. Walking humbly with God means allowing God your Father to take you by the hand and lead you. But too often we want to race off ahead of our loving Father, tearing our hand from his and running frantically in all directions. We don't want to miss anything. We want to experience everything that this life has to offer, so we run here and there in search of happiness—but we are always left yearning for something more.

If we will walk humbly with our God he will lead us by the hand to exactly who and what we need, to those people, things, and experiences he has designed and intended just for us, and this alone will be the cause of our deep fulfillment and happiness.

MEDITATION

What does humility mean to me? When I look at my life with the eyes of humility, where do I see God leading me this Advent?

PRAYER

God of joy, during these sometimes busy days of Advent, I keep your presence before my eyes. My heart is filled with joy for all you have done. You know the very depths of my soul, yet you love me with a tenderness that is beyond compare.

Wednesday of the Third Week of Advent

ISAIAH 45:6B–8, 18, 21B–25; LUKE 7:18B–23

"ARE YOU THE ONE WHO IS TO COME?"

. . . .

When the men had come to him, they said, "John the Baptist has
sent us to you to ask, 'Are you the one who is to come, or are we to
wait for another?'" And he answered them, "Go and tell John what
you have seen and heard: the blind receive their sight, the lame
walk, the lepers are cleansed, the deaf hear, the dead are raised, the
poor have good news brought to them. And blessed is anyone
who takes no offense at me."

(Luke 7:20, 22–23)

. . . .

REFLECTION

Is Jesus still relevant?

Gather all the books that have been written about the life and
teachings of Jesus. Add to them all the artwork Christian life has

inspired. Now consider all the music inspired by Christ, and the fact that the Church nurtured the development of the arts for centuries. Christianity is the moral foundation upon which America and many other nations built themselves.

Now consider the fact that prior to Christ walking the earth there was never any such thing as a hospital. Where were the sick when Jesus walked the earth? They were on the side of the road, left there to rot and die by relatives who feared for their own health.

How is it that we have also collectively forgotten that until the Church introduced education for the masses, there was never any such thing as an education for the common man? Education was only for the nobility until the Church introduced the idea that every person deserved an education.

All of these represent aspects of the measurable impact Christ has had on human history. And yet, these are all just dim reflections of the person who was and is Jesus Christ. Adding all of these together is still nothing compared to the impact Christ can have on your life, on my life. All the worldly success of Christ and the Church are

insignificant compared to the change Christ wants to have in you
and in your life.

MEDITATION

How well do I know the history of the Catholic Church? In what
ways can I start to increase my knowledge not only of the Church,
but also of Jesus Christ?

PRAYER

God of joy, during these sometimes busy days of Advent, I keep your
presence before my eyes. My heart is filled with joy for all you have
done. You know the very depths of my soul, yet you love me with a
tenderness that is beyond compare.

DON'T HOLD BACK—BE HOLY!

Sing, O barren one who did not bear;

burst into song and shout,

you who have not been in labor!

For the children of the desolate woman will be more

than the children of her that is married, says the LORD.

Enlarge the site of your tent,

and let the curtains of your habitations be stretched out;

do not hold back; lengthen your cords

and strengthen your stakes.

...

For your Maker is your husband,

the LORD of hosts is his name;

the Holy One of Israel is your Redeemer,

the God of the whole earth he is called.

(Isaiah 54:1–2, 5)

. . . .

REFLECTION

Many people falsely believe that if you want to be holy, you are not allowed to enjoy life. Some believe to be holy you have to run away from the world. Others think you have to be in church on your knees praying all day. Still others believe to be holy you have to walk around with a halo, that you're not allowed to smile, or have any fun, or enjoy yourself at all. They think to be holy you have to despise everything of this world and walk around with a stoic look on your face.

These are all the very unnatural and unattractive ideas that the world proclaims about holiness. The world ridicules holiness. The world pities the saints, saying, "Oh, he could have been so much more!" or "She had so much potential!" Let me assure you, it is not the saints who need our pity.

Those who respond to God's call to holiness are the most joyful people in history. They have a richer, more abundant experience of life, and they love more deeply than most people can ever imagine. They enjoy life—all of life Even in the midst of suffering they are able to maintain a peace and joy that are independent of the happenings and circumstances surrounding them.

Holiness doesn't stifle us; it sets us free.

MEDITATION

Do I see myself as a holy person? Why or why not? Can I believe that being holy can make me a happier person?

PRAYER

God of joy, during these sometimes busy days of Advent, I keep your presence before my eyes. My heart is filled with joy for all you have done. You know the very depths of my soul, yet you love me with a tenderness that is beyond compare.

Isaiah 56:1–3a, 6–8; John 5:33–36

SHARE YOUR LIGHT WITH THE WORLD
. . . .

John was a burning and shining lamp, and you were willing to
rejoice for a while in his light. But I have a testimony greater than
John's. The works that the Father has given me to complete,
the very works that I am doing, testify on my behalf that
the Father has sent me.

(John 5:35–36)
. . . .

REFLECTION

Within each of us there is a light. It is the light of God, and when it
shines it reflects not only the wonder of God but also the greatness
of the human spirit. We live in difficult times. I pray that we never
become fearful, but rather we turn our focus to nurturing the light
within us. I hope we allow that light within us to be nourished and

to grow. Darkness has one enemy that it can never defeat, and that is light. Let your light shine!

As we reflect on our brief and precious lives, let us also remember that they are but a transition to a long and blissful eternity. Teresa of Avila encourages us, "Remember you have only one soul; that you have only one death to die; that you have only one life, which is short and has to be lived by you alone; and there is only one glory, which is eternal. If you do this, there will be a great many things about which you care nothing."

It is for you to find your place in the history of humanity. Nobody can do it for you. It is a work that will be left undone unless you do it yourself. The world doesn't need another Mother Teresa. The Church doesn't need another Francis of Assisi. The world needs you. The Church needs you. Mother Teresa had a role to play in God's plan, and she played it. Francis had a mission to fulfill in God's plan, and he fulfilled it. Now it falls to you to find your role, your place.

MEDITATION

What is my role to play within the Church? What is my mission to the world? How can the light within guide my steps along the pathway of God's plan for me?

PRAYER

God of joy, during these sometimes busy days of Advent, I keep your presence before my eyes. My heart is filled with joy for all you have done. You know the very depths of my soul, yet you love me with a tenderness that is beyond compare.

Saturday of the Third Week of Advent

GENESIS 49:2, 8–10; MATTHEW 1:1–17

GOD HAS CREATED ME FOR A DEFINITE SERVICE

. . . .

Judah, your brothers shall praise you; your hand shall be on the neck of your enemies; your father's sons shall bow down before you. The scepter shall not depart from Judah, nor the ruler's staff from between his feet, until tribute comes to him; and the obedience of the peoples is his.

(Genesis 49:8, 10)

. . . .

REFLECTION

If you could change anything about the world, what would it be? The world is the way it is today because of people like you and me. Our thoughts, words, actions, and inaction have all contributed to create the world of today. What would the world be like if we multiplied your life by seven billion?

To have a global and historic impact, act locally. Whatever change you desire for the world, create that change in your own life. You are here for a purpose. Seek it out. Hunt it down. The greatest misery is to be purposeless. The great depression of our age is not economic, but spiritual. Our spiritual poverty is rooted in our purposelessness.

The words of John Henry Newman echo in my heart:

> God has created me to do him some definite service. He has committed some work to me which he has not committed to another. I have my mission. I may never know it in this life, but I shall be told it in the next. I am a link in a chain, a bond of connection between persons. He has not created me for naught. I shall do good—I shall do his work. I shall be an angel of peace, a preacher of truth in my own place while not intending it, if I do but keep his commandments. Therefore I will trust him; whatever I am, I can never be thrown away.

If we wish to speak effectively to the modern world about God, the Christian life, and the Catholic Church, we must be thriving, blossoming, and flourishing in this life.

MEDITATION

What do my thoughts say about me? Is there something good I can do locally in my home, neighborhood, or parish that can have an impact on the world?

PRAYER

God of joy, during these sometimes busy days of Advent, I keep your presence before my eyes. My heart is filled with joy for all you have done. You know the very depths of my soul, yet you love me with a tenderness that is beyond compare.

Year A: Isaiah 7:10–14; Romans 1:1–7; Matthew 1:18–24

Year B: 2 Samuel 7:1–5, 8b–12, 14a, 16; Romans 16:25–27; Luke 1:26–38

Year C: Micah 5:1–4a; Hebrews 10:5–10; Luke 1:39–45

NOTHING IS IMPOSSIBLE WITH GOD

Now to God who is able to strengthen you according to my gospel and the proclamation of Jesus Christ, according to the revelation of the mystery that was kept secret for long ages but is now disclosed, and through the prophetic writings is made known to all the Gentiles, according to the command of the eternal God, to bring about the obedience of faith—to the only wise God, through Jesus Christ, to whom be the glory for ever! Amen.

(Romans 16:25–27)

REFLECTION

The authentic life begins with the simple desire to be who God created us to be and cooperate with God by playing the part he has designed for us in human history. The adventure of salvation begins when we stop asking, "What's in it for me?" and turn humbly to God in our hearts and ask, "How may I serve? What work do you wish for me to do with my life? What is your will for my life?"

Every generation turns its back on God in its own way. Our modern era has revolted violently against the idea of "God's will." Desperate to maintain the illusion of being in control of their lives, many modern Christians have either turned their backs on God or created a new spiritual rhetoric that allows them to determine selectively God's will for their lives. And yet, it is the very surrendering of our own will to God's designs that characterizes the whole Christian struggle. The spiritual life is primarily concerned with this single dynamic of turning our individual will over to God.

God doesn't call you to live an authentic life in order to stifle or control you. He invites you to live an authentic life so that, from an infinite number of possibilities you can become the-best-version-of-yourself. By calling you to live an authentic life, God is saying, "Be all I create you to be."

MEDITATION

What is God's will for me? What implications does this have for my life right now, and on my efforts to live an authentic life?

PRAYER

The prayer for this week is based on Luke 1:34–35, 37–38: "The angel said to Mary, 'The Holy Spirit will come upon you, and the power of the Most High will overshadow you; therefore the child to be born will be holy; he will be called Son of God. For nothing will be impossible with God.' Then Mary said, 'Here am I, the servant of the Lord; let it be with me according to your word.' Then the angel departed from her." The birth of Jesus is near, and as we enter this final week of Advent, we reflect on the love of Christ through the experience of Mary, his mother.

God of love, as I come to the end of this Advent season, my heart is ready to celebrate the birth of Jesus. I join with Mary in saying, "Here am I, the servant of the Lord; let it be with me according to your word." Nothing is impossible with you, O God.

YOUR LIFE WILL CHANGE WHEN YOUR HABITS CHANGE

. . . .

The angel of the Lord appeared to the woman and said to her, "Although you are barren, having borne no children, you shall conceive and bear a son. Now be careful not to drink wine or strong drink, or to eat anything unclean, for you shall conceive and bear a son. No razor is to come on his head, for the boy shall be a nazirite to God from birth. It is he who shall begin to deliver Israel from the hand of the Philistines."

(Judges 13:3–5)

. . . .

REFLECTION

What are your habits? What are the things you do every day, every week, every month? Are your habits helping you become a-better-version-of-yourself or are they self-diminishing?

If you can tell me what your habits are, I can tell you what sort of person you are. Socrates, Aristotle, Thomas Aquinas, and Ignatius of Loyola established that habits create character. Good habits create good character, and bad habits create poor character. From a person's habits it is easy to deduce what his or her future will be like, because habits create character, and your character is your destiny. The good character created by good habits in turn creates a prosperous future. The bad character created by bad habits in turn creates misery in your future. Your character is your destiny in the workplace, in relationships, and in eternity.

Most people live in the misguided fantasy that one day they will wake up and suddenly their lives will be magically different. It doesn't happen. These people grow old and die waiting. Others live in the illusion that if they make more money, get a new car, buy a bigger house, get a promotion, or vacation in the Bahamas, then their lives will change. This doesn't work either.

Our lives change when our habits change. How would you like your life to be different this year than it was last year? How will this change come about?

MEDITATION

Which of my habits are helping me to become the-best-version-of-myself? Which habits are moving away from becoming the person God created me to be?

PRAYER

God of love, as I come to the end of this Advent season, my heart is ready to celebrate the birth of Jesus. I join with Mary in saying, "Here am I, the servant of the Lord; let it be with me according to your word." Nothing is impossible with you, O God.

Tuesday of the Fourth Week of Advent

ISAIAH 7:10–14; LUKE 1:26–38

A TIRED CULTURE LONGS
FOR GOD'S WORD

. . . .

Again the LORD spoke to Ahaz, saying, Ask a sign of the LORD your
God; let it be deep as Sheol or high as heaven. But Ahaz said, I will
not ask, and I will not put the Lord to the test. Then Isaiah said:
"Hear then, O house of David! Is it too little for you to weary mor-
tals, that you weary my God also?…"

(Isaiah 7:10–13)

. . . .

REFLECTION

Those of us who call ourselves Christian do so because we believe
that the life and teachings of Jesus Christ are the personification of
truth, sincerity, and authenticity, and in a practical sense, simply the
best way to live. If we are correct in this belief, and if the people of

the twenty-first century really are hungering for authenticity and the best way to live, then as Christians we must ask ourselves questions such as: Why are more people not enthusiastically embracing Christianity? Why, in fact, are so many people so hostile toward Christ and his Church?

I sense it is because the people of today believe that Christians, Christianity, and perhaps Catholics in particular are as much a part of this culture of appearance and deception as anyone else. People's desire for truth has not diminished, but they have become wary, doubtful, skeptical, and sadly, even cynical in their search for truth. To be honest, I cannot blame them for their attitude. I do not agree with their position, but I understand it. And perhaps more important, I can see how they arrived at that place of philosophical confusion and theological desolation.

The cause of much of this confusion is the unprecedented proliferation of words, symbols, images, and every manner of communication in the latter part of the twentieth century. People are tired; they are worn out, overloaded with information, and overwhelmed with the social, political, and economic climate. They are not striving to thrive; they are merely trying to survive. This is a tired culture.

MEDITATION

In what or in whom do I see truth? What is my source of comfort when the world wears me down?

PRAYER

God of love, as I come to the end of this Advent season, my heart is ready to celebrate the birth of Jesus. I join with Mary in saying, "Here am I, the servant of the Lord; let it be with me according to your word." Nothing is impossible with you, O God.

Song of Solomon 2:8–14; Luke 1:39–45

TO BE CATHOLIC IS TO BE LOVE IN ACTION

. . . .

My beloved speaks and says to me:

"Arise, my love, my fair one,

and come away;

for now the winter is past,

the rain is over and gone.

The flowers appear on the earth;

the time of singing has come,

and the voice of the turtledove

is heard in our land.

The fig tree puts forth its figs,

and the vines are in blossom;

they give forth fragrance.

Arise, my love, my fair one,

and come away.

(Song of Solomon 2:10–13)

. . . .

REFLECTION

As Catholics at the dawn of the twenty-first century, we are in the midst of a serious identity crisis. From where will we draw the guidance and inspiration to reestablish a vibrant Catholic identity in the world? At supper with his disciples for the last time, Jesus himself offered an answer to this question. His words are as fresh and relevant today as they were twenty centuries ago: "I give you a new commandment: Love one another. As I have loved you, so you should also love one another. This is how all will know that you are my disciples, if you have love for one another." (John 13:34–35)

The love that the life and teaching of Jesus Christ invite us to experience is real and relevant in every place and time, and the world is waiting for us to embody it. It is not a love of words and theories, but a love of action. It can be expressed in something as simple as helping someone in need, communicating our gratitude, feeding the hungry, or comforting the lonely.

How I wish that when people discovered you or I are Catholic, they could immediately conclude that we are honest, hardworking, generous, loving, joyful, compassionate, temperate, humble, disciplined, prayerful, and generally in love with life. You wouldn't need too many people like this to develop a positive reputation for Catholicism in a local community. I pray that God will transform you and me into Catholics of that caliber.

MEDITATION

In what ways do I show my love for God? For myself? For others?

PRAYER

God of love, as I come to the end of this Advent season, my heart is ready to celebrate the birth of Jesus. I join with Mary in saying, "Here am I, the servant of the Lord; let it be with me according to your word." Nothing is impossible with you, O God.

Thursday of the Fourth Week of Advent

GENESIS 17:3–9; JOHN 8:51–59

A COVENANT FOR LIFE

. . . .

Then Abram fell on his face; and God said to him, "I will establish

my covenant between me and you, and your offspring after you

throughout their generations, for an everlasting covenant, to be

God to you and to your offspring after you. And I will give to you,

and to your offspring after you, the land where you are now an

alien, all the land of Canaan, for a perpetual holding;

and I will be their God."

(Genesis 17: 3, 7–8)

. . . .

REFLECTION

The great minds of every era have grappled with universal and
enduring questions: Who am I? Where did I come from? What am I
here for? How do I do it? Where am I going? All of these questions

lead from (and back to) the question that has preoccupied humanity from the very beginning: What is the best way to live? The more people who ask this question and rigorously pursue an answer to it, the more dynamic and vibrant a society will be.

Every culture is the fruit of the ideas and attitudes of its people. These ideas and attitudes come together in both people and cultures to form philosophies. Every day you make hundreds of decisions. Some of these decisions affect what you eat and what you wear, while others affect the very direction of your life. In every case, these decisions are determined by your personal philosophy.

Today, there is little philosophical rigor in our culture. The way we consume information leads us to think less and less about more and more. We spend much of our time fixated on secondary questions (usually related to controversial and sensational issues) and very little time exploring the primary questions about our brief stay here on earth. This is why many of the philosophies we live our lives in allegiance to are absorbed through the culture rather than the result of any well-thought-out approach to life.

MEDITATION

What is my philosophy of life? Do I see God at the center of life's big questions? Have I established a covenant with God in relation to my life?

PRAYER

God of love, as I come to the end of this Advent season, my heart is ready to celebrate the birth of Jesus. I join with Mary in saying, "Here am I, the servant of the Lord; let it be with me according to your word." Nothing is impossible with you, O God.

Friday of the Fourth Week of Advent

JEREMIAH 20:10–13; JOHN 10:31–42

"THE FATHER IS IN ME AND I AM IN THE FATHER"

. . . .

The Jews took up stones again to stone him. Jesus answered, "If I am not doing the works of my Father, then do not believe me. But if I do them, even though you do not believe me, believe the works, so that you may know and understand that the Father is in me and I am in the Father."

(John 10:31, 34–38)

. . . .

REFLECTION

There is a desire within each of us to live an authentic life. We genuinely want to be true to ourselves. At times, we have perhaps resolved to live such a life with all the fervor we could muster. But distracted by the sweet seduction of pleasure and possessions, we have wandered from the narrow path. We know the truth, but we lack the discipline and strength of character to align the actions of our lives with that truth (cf. Matthew 26:41). We have given ourselves over to a thousand different whims, cravings, and fantasies. Our lives have become merely a distortion of the truth we know and profess. We know the human family's need for kindness, compassion, generosity, forgiveness, acceptance, freedom, and love, but we have divided our hearts with a thousand contradictions and compromises.

At every moment, the entire modern world kneels before us, begging, pleading, beckoning for some brave man or woman to come forward and lead them with the example of an authentic life.

In many respects our age is one of abundance, but amid this abundance (which at times may seem all prevailing) there remains a great hunger in the people of today. We have a universal hunger for the authentic, a longing to be and become and experience all we are capable of and created for. Everything good in the future—for ourselves, our marriages, our families, our communities, our Church, our nation, and humanity—depends on whether or not we will follow this longing.

MEDITATION

Do I see my work as a joy or as drudgery? How does my work bring me closer to God? Is God calling me to a change in my life?

PRAYER

God of love, as I come to the end of this Advent season, my heart is ready to celebrate the birth of Jesus. I join with Mary in saying, "Here am I, the servant of the Lord; let it be with me according to your word." Nothing is impossible with you, O God.

Saturday of the Fourth Week of Advent

EZEKIEL 37:21–28; JOHN 11:45–56

YOU ARE MY PEOPLE

. . . .

Thus says the Lord GOD: I will take the people of Israel from the nations among which they have gone, and will gather them from every quarter, and bring them to their own land. I will make them one nation in the land, on the mountains of Israel; and one king shall be king over them all.... I will make a covenant of peace with them; it shall be an everlasting covenant with them; and I will bless them and multiply them, and will set my sanctuary among them forevermore. My dwelling place shall be with them; and I will be their God, and they shall be my people.

(Ezekiel 37:21–22, 26–27)

. . . .

REFLECTION

We are at a turning point in human history. Most people do not recognize it because they are so consumed with their own selfish desires and the trivial happenings of their daily lives. What is needed is a handful of great spiritual leaders to direct the human family during this critical period of transition. The modern western empire is in decline. It will soon die. It's not the end of the world. It's not the end of humanity. It's just the beginning of a new era. A new civilization will emerge. And what will this new civilization be like? That is entirely up to the stories we tell, listen to, and live.

Pope Benedict XVI wrote, "The crucial question is whether there are saints who…are ready to effect something new and living." As Christians, we are called to holiness, a life of prayer and virtue. We are called to be saints.

The best thing you can do for yourself is to become the-best-version-of-yourself. The best thing you can do for your spouse, your children, your friends, your Church, your nation, and God is to become the-best-version-of-yourself. Catholicism is not a lifeless set of rules and regulations; it is a lifestyle. Catholicism is a dynamic way of life designed by God to help you explore your incredible potential.

Find your place in salvation history. Be a saint. Be yourself. Perfectly yourself.

MEDITATION

What have I discovered about my faith during this Advent? What must change in my life in order for me to immerse myself in Catholicism?

PRAYER

God of love, as I come to the end of this Advent season, my heart is ready to celebrate the birth of Jesus. I join with Mary in saying, "Here am I, the servant of the Lord; let it be with me according to your word." Nothing is impossible with you, O God.

Christmas Day

Isaiah 52:7–10; Hebrews 1:1–6; John 1:1–18

LET THE CELEBRATION BEGIN!

· ·

In the beginning was the Word, and the Word was with God, and
the Word was God. He was in the beginning with God. All things
came into being through him, and without him not one thing came
into being. What has come into being in him was life, and the life
was the light of all people. The light shines in the darkness, and the
darkness did not overcome it.

(John 1:1–5)

· ·

REFLECTION

The spirit of Catholicism is predominantly one of celebration, which
is the genius and the fundamental orientation of our faith. At this
moment in history, both life and faith are being attacked with the full
force of a culture racing toward self-destruction. These are direct
attacks on the essence of the human person.

I believe the best way to defend life is to celebrate life. I believe the best way to celebrate life is to live our own lives to the fullest—to embrace life with arms wide open, to lay our lives enthusiastically at the service of humanity, to love deeply the people who cross our paths, and above all, to embrace our God. Life should never be wasted—not one moment—because life is precious.

I believe the best way to defend the faith is to celebrate our faith. The best way to celebrate Catholicism is to live the faith more fully with each passing day, allowing it to reach into every corner of our lives. When Catholicism is the foundation of our family life, our social life, our intellectual life, our spiritual life, our community life, and our professional life, then we will have established an integrated life, a life of integrity. That unity of life will speak more powerfully than any words ever could. And if just a handful of people in one place and at one time will give their whole selves to seeking, discovering, embracing, and living this life, they will change the whole course of human history.

What are we celebrating as a culture? What are you celebrating? You have become the person you are because of the things you celebrate. Our culture has become what it is because of the things we celebrate.

You can celebrate anything you wish. You can celebrate life and faith. You can celebrate love and honesty, mercy and forgiveness, kindness and generosity. You can celebrate truth, beauty, goodness, and redemption. On the other hand, you can celebrate destruction and paganism. You can celebrate hatred and violence, selfishness and greed, contempt and disrespect. You can celebrate perversion, corruption, pride, deceit, and condemnation. But one thing is certain: We become what we celebrate. This is the one immutable truth found in the life of every person who has ever lived. We become what we celebrate. It is true not only of the life of a person but also of the life of a family. It is true of the life of a nation, and it is true of the life of the Church.

Let the celebration begin.

MEDITATION

What will I celebrate today and all throughout this Christmas season? How can I extend this celebration into every moment of my life?

PRAYER FOR CHRISTMAS DAY

Today I sing with the angels, "Glory to God in the highest, and on earth, peace to all of good will!" Jesus, you are the light of the world, who shines through the darkness of our days. This Christmas season and throughout the year, I will be your disciple and follow in your footsteps, bringing light to all God's creation. Amen.

NOTES

The reflections in this book are drawn from *Rediscover Catholicism: A Spiritual Guide to Living with Passion and Purpose* (Cincinnati: Beacon, 2011). Minor alterations have been made for the purpose of this edition. The page numbers from which the passages are drawn are listed below.

Introduction: pp. 17–25

First Week of Advent

Sunday: p. 42; **Monday:** p. 59; **Tuesday:** pp. 31–32; **Wednesday:** pp. 29–30; **Thursday:** pp. 122–123; **Friday:** pp. 72–73; **Saturday:** pp. 61–62

Second Week of Advent

Sunday: pp. 55–56; **Monday:** p. 41; **Tuesday:** pp. 47–48; **Wednesday:** p. 89; **Thursday:** pp. 18–19; **Friday:** p. 90; **Saturday:** pp. 51–52

Third Week of Advent

Sunday: pp. 115–116; **Monday:** p. 47; **Tuesday:** pp. 125–126;

Wednesday: p. 46; **Thursday:** p. 76; **Friday:** pp. 140;

Saturday: p. 143

Fourth Week of Advent

Sunday: p. 69; **Monday:** pp. 127; **Tuesday:** p. 31;

Wednesday: p. 57; **Thursday:** p. 35; **Friday:** p. 33;

Saturday: pp. 141–142

Christmas Day: pp. 65–66

APPENDIX

. . . .

Ten-year Cycle of Lectionary Readings for the Sundays in Advent

Year A—2013, 2016, 2019

First Week: Isaiah 2:1–5; Romans 13:11–14; Matthew 24:37–44

Second Week: Isaiah 11:1–10; Romans 15:4–9; Matthew 3:1–12

Third Week: Isaiah 35:1–6a, 10; James 5:7–10; Matthew 11:2–11

Fourth Week: Isaiah 7:10–14; Romans 1:1–7; Matthew 1:18–24

Year B—2011, 2014, 2017, 2020

First Week: Isaiah 63:16b–17, 19b, 64:2–7; 1 Corinthians 1:3–9; Mark 13:33–37

Second Week: Isaiah 40:1–5, 9–11; 2 Peter 3:8–14; Mark 1:1–8

Third Week: Isaiah 61:1–2a, 10–11; 1 Thessalonians 5:16–24; John 1:6–8, 19–28

Fourth Week: 2 Samuel 7:1–5, 8b–12, 14a, 16; Romans 16:25–27; Luke 1:26–38

Year C—2012, 2015, 2018, 2021

First Week: Jeremiah 33:14–16; 1 Thessalonians 3:12—4:2; Luke 21:25–28, 34–36

Second Week: Baruch 5:1–9; Philippians 1:4–6. 8–11; Luke 3:1–6

Third Week: Zephaniah 3:14–18a; Philippians 4:4–7; Luke 3:10–18

Fourth Week: Micah 5:1–4a; Hebrews 10:5–10; Luke 1:39–45

ABOUT THE AUTHOR

Matthew Kelly is a *New York Times* best-selling author of fourteen books, a world-renowned speaker, and a business consultant to more than thirty-five Fortune 500 companies. His titles include *Rediscover Catholicism: Journeying Toward Our Spiritual North Star, The Rhythm of Life: Living Every Day with Passion and Purpose,* and *Building Better Families: A Practical Guide to Raising Amazing Children.* To learn more about his work, visit DynamicCatholic.com.